TOO MUCH TRASH IN THE PARK

By

Thomas Conti

Dedicated To

our son Thomas Conti Jr. - Love, Mom and Dad

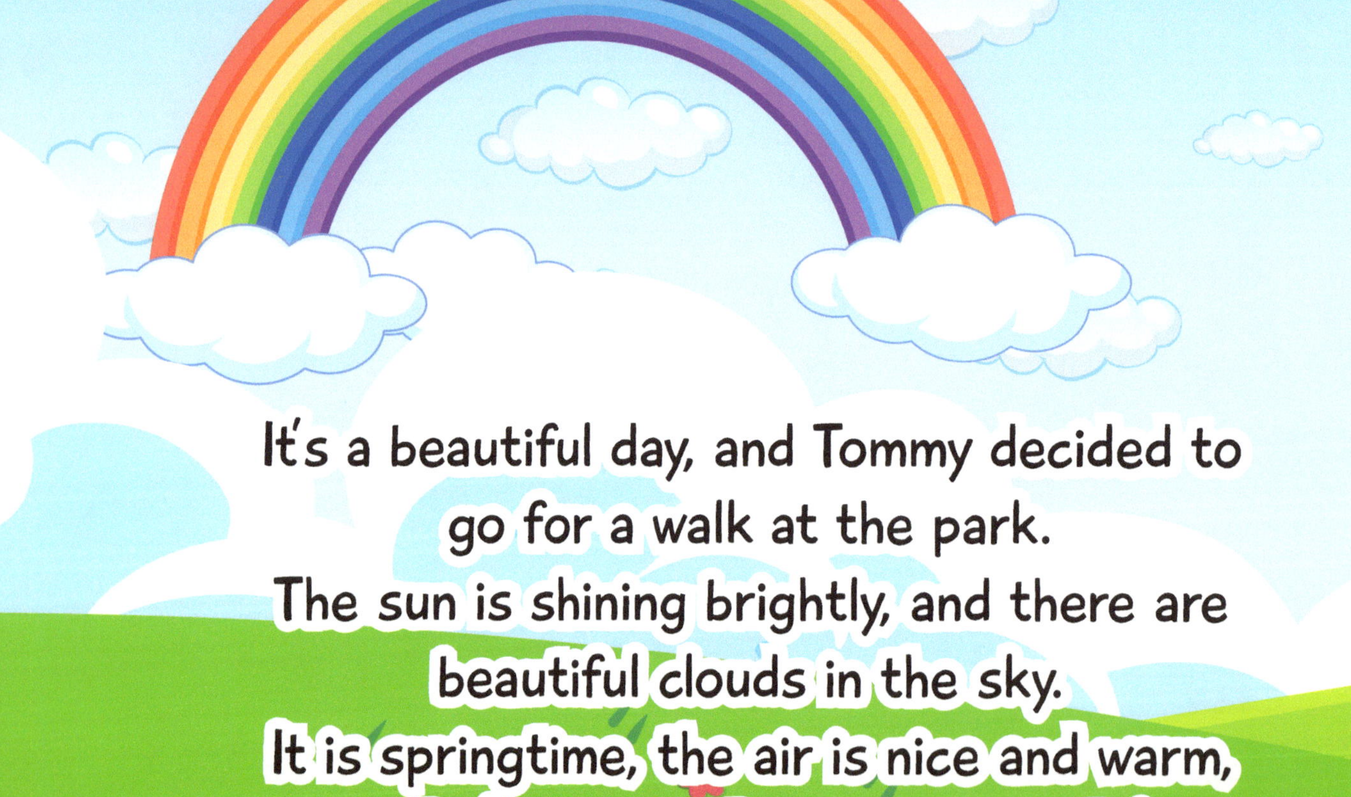

It's a beautiful day, and Tommy decided to
go for a walk at the park.
The sun is shining brightly, and there are
beautiful clouds in the sky.
It is springtime, the air is nice and warm,
and it's a great day to be outside!
The outdoors bring many exciting opportunities,
and many adventures are awaiting!

Bees can be seen buzzing around
from flower to flower.
They are collecting pollen to make
into sweet and delicious honey.
Honey bees work hard for their
hive and their queen.
Unknowingly, bees polinate our plants and
help make fruits and vegetables for us.

Tommy loves seeing nature and enjoys
taking walks in the parks.
Every time there is a nice day, Tommy is outside.
The more parks Tommy visits the closer
he feels to nature.
Tommy is realizing that we need to
value the outdoors.

Tommy has gotten worried though, because
he keeps seeing trash in this park.
He starts to see how the trash is
hurting nature.
This saddens Tommy who sees how the
trash is affecting the animals.
He decides that it is up to him to help
save the parks.

Tommy thinks to himself,
"There's too much trash in the park."
He continues walking and looking around
thinking, "This trash is creating trouble
for the animals and insects."

Tommy decides to go to work just
as the worker bees.
He gathers the supplies he needs to
complete his good deed.
After putting on his new pair of gloves and
grabbing a few trash bags he gets to work.
Any signs of trash in the park that
Tommy saw, he was sure to clean it up.

While cleaning the park, Tommy got
even closer to nature.
He got to appreciate caterpillars, bugs,
and animals of all kinds.
Even some things he had never seen
before while walking at the park.
Nature was starting to come out more
now that the park was getting cleaner.

Later that year, Tommy went back to
the same park and took a walk.
The trails were surrounded by colorful
flowers in full bloom and fragrent.
Beautiful butterflies began to fly all
around him covering the trail.
He continued walking and the butterflies
were every he looked.

Tommy knew the butterflies were the same
caterpillars he had seen before.
The butterflies were thanking him for
cleaning up their home.
By cleaning up the park earlier that year,
he made it a better place for nature.
Tommy learned that he could help nature
by picking up trash one piece at a time.

The End!